WORLD BANK DISCUSSION PAPER NO. 395

School Enrollment Decline in Sub-Saharan Africa

Beyond the Supply Constraint

Joseph W. B. Bredie
Girindre K. Beeharry

The World Bank
Washington, D.C.

Discussion Papers present results of country analysis or research that are circulated to encourage discussion and comment within the development community. The typescript of this paper therefore has not been prepared in accordance with the procedures appropriate to formal printed texts, and the World Bank accepts no responsibility for errors. Some sources cited in this paper may be informal documents that are not readily available.

The findings, interpretations, and conclusions expressed in this paper are entirely those of the author(s) and should not be attributed in any manner to the World Bank, to its affiliated organizations, or to members of its Board of Executive Directors or the countries they represent. The World Bank does not guarantee the accuracy of the data included in this publication and accepts no responsibility for any consequence of their use. The boundaries, colors, denominations, and other information shown on any map in this volume do not imply on the part of the World Bank Group any judgment on the legal status of any territory or the endorsement or acceptance of such boundaries.

The material in this publication is copyrighted. Requests for permission to reproduce portions of it should be sent to the Office of the Publisher at the address shown in the copyright notice above. The World Bank encourages dissemination of its work and will normally give permission promptly and, when the reproduction is for noncommercial purposes, without asking a fee. Permission to copy portions for classroom use is granted through the Copyright Clearance Center, Inc., Suite 910, 222 Rosewood Drive, Danvers, Massachusetts 01923, U.S.A.

ISSN: 0259-210X

Joseph W. B. Bredie is senior education specialist in the Human Development II Group of the World Bank's Africa Region. Girindre K. Beeharry is a young professional in the Human Development Group of the World Bank's Latin America and the Caribbean Region.

Library of Congress Cataloging-in-Publication Data

Bredie, Joseph W. B.
    School enrollment decline in Sub-Saharan Africa : beyond the
supply constraint / Joseph W.B. Bredie, Girindre K. Beeharry.
       p.   cm. — (World Bank discussion paper, ISSN 0259-210X ; no.
395)
   ISBN 0-8213-4312-2
   1. School enrollment—Africa, Sub-Saharan.   2. Education,
Elementary—Africa, Sub-Saharan.   3. Family—Africa, Sub-Saharan—
Economic conditions.   I. Beeharry, Girindre K., 1967–   .
II. Title.   III. Series: World Bank discussion papers ; 395.
LC137.S73B74   1998
372.12'1967—dc21   98-34812
                                          CIP

Contents

FOREWORD

The overarching objective of the World Bank's assistance to Sub-Saharan African countries is poverty reduction through sustained economic growth at a high level, with a pro-poor distribution, and improved social services. Past experience from both industrialized and newly industrialized countries show that a minimum level of educational attainment has been a pre-requisite for the success of such a strategy. Therefore, the current low levels of education development, particularly with respect to primary education and especially for girls, is of great concern. No industrialized or newly industrialized country achieved sustained growth with adult literacy rates as low as those found today in the majority of sub-Saharan African countries. Moreover, the development of primary education has stagnated, or even declined, in a number of countries since the early 1980s.

To help reverse this stagnation, we need to understand better what is happening. This paper provides a contribution in this regard. It looks at the constraints in the demand for schooling and suggests that one of the possible reasons for the stagnation is that households are concerned about the high cost and uncertain benefits of schooling. The authors suggest that we need to do more to reduce the direct and opportunity cost of schooling and to stimulate the demand for schooling.

As the Bank moves vigorously to assist countries develop programs to accelerate their development of education, especially at the primary level and for girls, it becomes very important for us to better understand the factors which determine whether parents enroll their children at school and, in case they do, whether they will maintain them at school. This type of information will be particularly important for the success of emerging approaches based on demand side financing.

Birger Fredriksen
Sector Director
Human Development
Africa Region

iv

ABSTRACT

This paper examines the likely causes for deteriorating enrollment rates in Africa. While a causal link is difficult to establish, several studies suggest that declining incomes and employment opportunities impact on household schooling decisions (i.e., household demand for education). The prevalent view that deterioration in school availability and quality are responsible for declining school enrollments in many African countries seems incomplete. One consequence of this finding is that the policy response to declining enrollments should not be restricted to building more schools and improving existing ones. Cost-reducing and demand-stimulating or financing measures should be considered as well. Analytical tools can help policy-makers assess which of the costs and benefits of education impact on household schooling decisions. While a comprehensive analysis, using demand for education regressions, is impractical because of data requirement, a simple private rates of return analysis can be a second-best diagnostic instrument to identify constraining factors in education demand.

ACKNOWLEDGEMENTS

We acknowledge with appreciation the enduring support of Ms. Ishrat Z. Husain for the regional study program on education-economy linkages which provided the resources for the preparation of this paper. We would also like to acknowledge the three external reviewers - Professor Keith Lewin, Professor Jerry R. Behrman and Professor Paul Bennell for their critical comments and their encouragement to publish the paper and contribute to the discussion on the demand for education in Africa. The comments of colleagues at the Bank, in particular Arvil Van Adams, Harry Patrinos and Herbert Bergman were also much appreciated

1. INTRODUCTION: ENROLLMENT STAGNATION

For almost two decades after independence, enrollments in primary school in sub-Saharan Africa grew remarkably fast. Continent-wide primary school enrollment rates rose from 36 in 1960, to 48 in 1970 and 68 in 1990.[1] Presumably, public and private investments in education were made in the belief that education is a fundamental human right, and essential for economic success. As long as education led to better-paid jobs, neither households nor governments had any reason to question the benefits of investments in education. However, the pace of investments in education lost momentum in several African countries in the mid-1980s. Between 1981 and 1991, primary enrollment rates declined[2] in at least fourteen[3] of the twenty-seven African countries surveyed. This came at the same time as macro-economic imbalances worsened.

A number of drastic changes in the economic environment caused the virtuous circle of education accumulation and economic growth to break down. Although there seems to be a strong correlation between economic deterioration and declines in enrollment, a causal link is difficult to establish. What can be said is that a number of African countries experienced a drop in households' disposable income, and a decline in employment prospects for educated workers. At the same time, there was a decline in the public resources allocated to the education sector, a decline in the quality of schools, and in enrollments. The general decline would be innocuous were education a good like any other, but under-investment in education is widely held to harm growth prospects.[4]

---

[1] Estimates vary from one source to the other, but all show the same sharp rise in primary enrollments.

[2] The possibility that the decline results purely from measurement errors is excluded. Measurement problems are known to exist but would not, alone, explain the consistent declines observed in such a representative sample of countries in the region over such a long period of time.

[3] Benin, Cameroon, the Central African Republic, Côte d'Ivoire, The Gambia, Guinea-Bissau, Kenya, Madagascar, Mali, Mozambique, Nigeria, Tanzania, Zambia, and Zimbabwe.

[4] Three lessons can be drawn from the growth literature: (i) the long-term growth perspectives of a country largely depend upon its initial human capital endowments - it is therefore important that these should be augmented; (ii) human capital has to be harnessed in some way if it is to participate effectively to the growth process; if it is being productively utilized, then returns to investments in education are likely to be high, and private agents are likely to engage readily in these investments; (iii) there is a clear role for public intervention in human capital accumulation inasmuch as private agents are likely to omit external economies from their cost-benefit analyses. The long-term growth prospects of the economy might be jeopardized if a slump in (private and public) investment in education is left unattended.

2. THE PREVAILING DIAGNOSIS: INSUFFICIENT BUDGET ALLOCATIONS

Kakwani, Makonnen, and van der Gaag (1990), suggested that fiscal retrenchment forced on by deteriorating economic conditions is the primary cause of the decline in enrollment rates. The link they make between worsening economic conditions and declining enrollments is mediated by declining education budgets. They found that the fiscal realignment, that several African countries had to undertake as part of economic adjustment, included a cut in government spending on education. This resulted in a decrease in both the quality and provision of schools. This decrease in quality and availability, in turn, was responsible for household dissatisfaction with primary education and their decision not to enroll their children. This view led to a widespread agreement that the education sector budget needs to be "protected" or excluded from fiscal retrenchment.

In several countries, however, maintaining the education sector budget did not solve the problem of declining enrollment rates. During the period 1981-91, primary enrollments decreased in fourteen countries and increased in thirteen countries in a sample of twenty-seven adjusting African countries.[5] For the sixteen countries for which data[6] were available, we find the following relation between primary school enrollment and real education spending per capita.

Table 1: Real Education Spending and Enrollment Rates

Primary enrollment rates	Number of countries with an increase in real per capita education spending	Number of countries with a decrease in real per capita education spending
Increases	1	6
Decreases	2	7
Decreases	3	13

Source: Authors (1997)

---

[5] For a few countries, there is some evidence for attributing the decline in enrollment rates to an increase in school or teacher rationing or to the failure of the education system to match the population growth. This is not the case for all of them, and some of these countries actually experience declines in absolute enrollments for which a shortage of schools or teachers cannot be blamed.

[6] Computed from the World Bank Stars Database; data reliability being problematic, other sources might yield a different picture.

Table 1 shows seven countries where enrollment rates and per capita expenditures both decreased, confirming the Kakwani *et al.* diagnosis. However, it also shows that enrollment rates decreased in two of the countries although the real per capita spending in education increased. Moreover, six countries saw a concurrent increase in enrollment rates and a decrease in real per capita spending on education.

The weak correlation between changes in education spending and enrollment rates does not seem to give strong support for the fiscal retrenchment diagnosis. Noss (1991), in his review of the literature on education enrollments and spending, also comments on the weak basis for the diagnosis. He contends that "country studies suggest that public education financing is not immediately and directly associated with enrollment rates ......evidence of reductions on public expenditures during adjustment is pervasive, but there is considerable uncertainty regarding the effects of declining public financing on education."

The absence of a robust correlation between education sector budgets and enrollments does not necessarily imply that they are actually disconnected. The weak correlation might, in certain cases, reflect the fact that the budgets are not effectively disbursed or utilized. While there are potential gains therefore to ensuring that budget allocations are adequate, it is even more important to ensure that funds reach the schools. This is demonstrated in the PRAGAP[7] experience in Madagascar. By ensuring that schools were adequately equipped and furnished to allow for satisfactory teaching and learning conditions, PRAGAP led to important enrollment increases. However, the PRAGAP experience also showed that adequate provisions in terms of supplies and teaching staff did not *entirely* solve the problem of enrollments. There were a significant number of school-age children in the communities participating in the PRAGAP scheme who still did not attend school.

Safeguarding public expenditures on education alone does not halt enrollment declines, not even when the funds effectively reach the schools. However, reduced public spending on education is widely held responsible for the decline in education enrollment. For that reason, increasing school availability and quality have been the primary measures taken to check the decline. The second generation of Bank's Sector Adjustment Loans, for instance, sought to maintain or increase real expenditures on education, and especially primary education, in a period of overall reduction of public expenditures.[8] However, the effectiveness of this policy response in terms of maintaining or increasing enrollments, remains to be established.

---

[7] Programme de Renforcement et d'Amélioration de la Gestion Administrative et Pédagogique, part of the Education Sector Reinforcement Project. PRAGAP schools saw an increase in new enrollments in grade 1 of about 33 percent, while intakes in non-PRAGAP schools increased at most by 3 percent.

[8] See Ribe and Carvalho (1990).

Focusing exclusively on availability and quality of schools is not sufficient to maintain enrollments. The studies on which this policy is based did not analyze if there is a link between, for instance, declining income and labor market demand and deteriorating enrollments. If these factors play a role in declining enrollments, then maintaining access and quality alone as suggested by these studies will not stem the decline. Noss, among others, notes that studies "seldom include indicators for factors (other than public education expenditures) that influence the demand for education, for example, income distribution, real and opportunity costs of education, and potential returns from education".

The studies seem to assume that there is a "natural" demand for education, or that since primary education is compulsory, parents will send their children to school. This assumption may have been acceptable during the 1960s and 1970s, but, the difficult economic conditions that have led to lower household incomes have made the (direct and opportunity) cost of education an important burden for many households. At the same time, the benefits of education in terms of increasing the chances of securing employment have also deteriorated because of fewer employment opportunities. Demand for education, even at primary level can no longer be taken for granted. A number of education sector studies report that parents find that education is no longer a worthwhile investment, and that expenses outweigh the potential benefits. For example, in Madagascar[9], when parents were asked the reason for not sending their children to school, the two main responses were: school is too expensive, and school curricula is not adapted to the reality of day-to-day life. In Mozambique,[10] parents complain that the cost of school-related items (clothing, in particular) as well as the cost of children's time, particularly in labor-intensive periods, can be prohibitive. In Tanzania,[11] parents do not send their children to school because, among other things, they get little value for money, because their children learn very little, and because the school-community relations are poor.

Failure to pay attention to demand when considering public investments in education may have several drawbacks. It may first and foremost result in a low response rate to an increase in the supply of school places. It may also result in a failure to improve equity if households that are targeted for enrolling their children, for example, rural poor, do not take advantage of the opportunities created because they cannot afford to do so. On the other hand, non-poor households who would have sent their children to public or private school anyway will more readily take advantage of the additional public school places created, further distorting equity. It may also result in a failure to improve efficiency if additional school places created are taken by repeaters instead of children who never attended school, but were targeted for enrollment.

---

[9] See Madagascar Poverty Assessment, Box 5.1, page 68.

[10] See Palme (1993).

[11] See Tadreg, 1993.

3. HOUSEHOLD DEMAND FOR EDUCATION

The studies reviewed in this chapter provide more systematic evidence that demand for education needs to be taken into account for efforts to reverse the decline in primary school enrollment in the region to succeed. They analyze various factors that are linked to economic conditions such as direct and opportunity costs, income and employment opportunities, and their association with households' schooling decisions.

The focus in the studies are the households since households are the ultimate decision-makers about the schooling of their children. Their choices in the aggregate determine enrollment levels.

There is growing empirical literature on the determinants of household demand for education in Africa. Interest in this question was originally prompted by the need to understand what the impact of the macroeconomic decline and subsequent changes in economic policy regimes in the 1980s was on the social sectors. The research showed that households take changing economic conditions into account in their decisions to allocate resources among members. The allocation of resources to the different members of the household are determined in view of the ultimate use of the resources. When these resources become scarce, as is the case when the economy deteriorates, essential items such as food, shelter and clothing may compete with uses for education. Households' willingness to invest in education can, in those cases, not be taken for granted. In view of this finding, subsequent studies began to pay closer attention to the determinants of household schooling choices. Three studies of this kind in two African countries, Côte d'Ivoire and Tanzania, are reviewed below.

Appleton on Côte d'Ivoire

Appleton (1991), was one of the first researchers to analyze data from a household survey to determine which variables significantly influence the schooling decisions for an African country. To appreciate the empirical nature of the findings, it is useful to look briefly at the design of the study and at the variables that were included. Appleton treats education as an investment good. He assumes that households will pay for education if they find that the present value of benefits outweighs the cost. Three sets of variables play a role in the households' schooling choices: schooling benefits, the cost of schooling; and the ability of the household to pay for schooling.

Appleton's assessment is that while there are benefits to schooling, the evidence that education brings returns to households depending on agriculture is less strong than for households with access to formal sector employment. It is therefore likely that the principal factors affecting schooling in rural settings are costs and household income, rather than future benefits.

In deciding how the cost of schooling influences enrollment decisions, Appleton takes into account direct costs (tuition, books, uniforms and travel), as well as indirect or opportunity costs. Opportunity costs or foregone income represent a significant part of the cost of schooling, particularly at the secondary and higher education levels. Foregone incomes are typically more difficult to measure for primary education.[12] However, in the region, opportunity cost of schooling can be substantial.[13] Opportunity cost is estimated on the basis of the wages a student would earn if he/she were working instead of attending school. Opportunity costs typically weigh more heavily on poor households. This would seem to be the case in the region but it is also true in industrial countries.[14]

Appleton also includes income as an explanatory variable in his demand for education equation. Even if households find that schooling brings returns and decide to enroll their child(ren), low-income households are rarely able to borrow to finance schooling. In such circumstances, household income is likely to be an important if not the sole source of funds for schooling. In those cases, the level of household income will play a key role in determining school attainment.

A few of the more important findings of the study are as follows. The level of economic welfare of the household, as measured by consumption per capita, increases the probability that their children enroll in school. However, the relationship between schooling probability and level of household consumption is not strong enough to predict enrollment on the basis of, say, income level. This might be taken to indicate that, other things being equal, targeting education by income levels in Côte d'Ivoire may not be very effective to improve equity. In urban areas, households that own and operate their own (non-agricultural) enterprises are less likely to school their children. This is an interesting and somewhat counter-intuitive finding since one could hypothesize that entrepreneurial parents would be more aware than others of the usefulness of knowledge and skills acquired at school. However, it may also be that the child's present-day contribution to the enterprise are perceived as being more valuable than the potential or future benefits from schooling. In rural areas, higher child wages (i.e. higher opportunity costs of children's time) have the effect of increasing the probability of boys dropping out, and decreasing the likelihood that girls will drop out.[15] This finding also confirms that households take income foregone into account and will take the children with a better potential to earn money immediately (boys in this case) out of school if they need the additional income. This finding could also be taken to mean that one potential lever to tackle gender equity would be through some form of action on opportunity costs.[16]

---

[12] See Bennell (1995).

[13] See Mason and Khandker on Tanzania (1996), and Burkina Faso, Post-Primary Education Project PAD(1996).

[14] See Barr (1993).

[15] See Annex for a discussion of opportunity costs for girls and boys in Madagascar in the context of explaining the absence of gender differences in enrollments.

[16] One such action could be to tailor the school calendar so that holidays coincide with labor-intensive periods.

Also, in rural areas, the likelihood that boys are in school decreases with the distance of the household to its wood fuel source.[17] A related finding of the study is that the greater the distance to the household drinking water source, the less likely it is that children complete their primary schooling. This finding may, however, be specific to the sample in this study because another analysis of performance on primary-leaving exams in Côte d'Ivoire provides no corroboration that distance to water sources influences academic performance. At the same time, these types of findings are increasingly being taken into account in rural education projects in specific countries where these issues have proven to play a role through, for instance, the provision of piped water as a potential lever for increasing enrollments.

In general, though, the findings of the study lend support to the hypothesis that household demand for education depends upon many more variables than just schooling availability and quality. Several policy implications can be drawn from the Appleton study. It may or may not be necessary to target household by income levels according to whether enrollment probabilities increase significantly or not with income. Similarly, in rural areas, it may be necessary to give incentives to households to help them send their boys to school who may otherwise be put in charge of collecting fuelwood or sent to work in the fields. It may not be easy to decide on specific policy interventions on the basis of a study such as Appleton's, but the study is very useful in that it demonstrates that the demand for education cannot be taken for granted and is likely to vary substantially on the basis of income, gender and or region. To achieve education for all in the region, the demand for education needs to be analyzed as part of sector work before investments projects are prepared.

De Vreyer on Côte d'Ivoire

De Vreyer (1993) also undertook a study of the determinants of demand for education in Côte d'Ivoire somewhat similar to the work done by Appleton. The study differs, however, in a number of ways. De Vreyer includes several additional variables: The employment category of the head of household which is likely to influence household schooling decisions; an indicator reflecting if the household produces cash crops with guaranteed prices; and, several infrastructure indicators (such as, distance to the nearest paved road, to public transportation, and to primary and secondary schools).

De Vreyer's analysis differs from Appleton's in yet another way. The study design takes explicit account of intra-household bargaining. To that effect, it includes variables such as the sex of the head of household, the relation of the child to the head of household, the order of birth of the child, the age of the head of household at the time of birth of the child, and the education and profession of the head of household.

The major findings of this study can be summarized as follows. The gender of the head of household matters. A male head favors boys' education more than a female head

---

[17] In the case discussed here, the author even finds this effect to be stronger than the issues of child wages.

does. An interesting finding is that female-headed households generally invest more in the education of children. De Vreyer also found that the age of the head of household at the time of birth of the child is significant. It seems that households invest less in the education of their first-born than in that of their other children. The educational attainment of the head of household is positively correlated with that of their offspring. More educated parents tend to invest more in education. Along similar lines, the study established that the occupation of the head of household is significant - a wage earner (and in particular, a civil servant) is more likely to invest more in the education of his or her children.

Two interesting findings that support the fact that households take cost and benefits of education into account are the following. The supply cost of educational services (including the distance from school) is negatively correlated with educational attainment. In other words, the cost of education determines the amount of education that households will select for their children. Income per head is strongly and positively correlated with educational attainment in urban areas: richer households tend to demand more schooling for their children than less well-off households.

Finally, geographic location matters - there is a difference of about nine years between the average educational attainment in Abidjan and in the Savannah. This difference in attainment between urban and rural areas is also closely linked with income and infrastructure disparities. Again, this suggests that the demand for education among rural households is lower than that of their urban counterparts because they tend to be poorer and have a limited infrastructural environment. A further refinement of geographic differences is that cash crop producers benefiting from guaranteed prices for their produce invest more in the education of their children.

De Vreyer, like Appleton, included variables that are related to access and quality of schooling. However, the findings suggest that non-school factors, such as level of parents' education, infrastructure, and income of households, have a significant impact on schooling decisions. It is the compounded impact of access, quality, costs and benefits that determine enrollment levels. Obtaining a measure of the relative weight of these variables is important to decide on the most appropriate type of intervention. One policy implication is that constructing more schools could possibly fail to increase educational attainment if not supported by demand stimulation or some other kind of support to the household. The latter could be in the form of education subsidies for the poorest, some form of gender-targeting, providing information about the benefits of education in rural areas, or reducing the cost of education. A more recent research study on demand for education in Tanzania, discussed below, simulates the effect of two such measures on enrollment probability.

Mason and Khandker on Tanzania

Mason and Khandker (1996) examined the determinants of enrollment in Tanzania. They also analyzed the reasons for late or over-age enrollments in primary and secondary schools. They undertook the research for the purpose of finding out what types of intervention can best improve performance in the education sector. Their approach was similar in that they analyzed data from household surveys and determined the relative importance of a number of variables on the demand for education. They carried the analysis further by actually simulating the impact on enrollment probabilities of different sets of policy measures.

The findings are presented by level of education. For primary education, the study findings can be summarized by saying that in the case of Tanzania, both access and cost influence demand. Constraints in the supply of primary schools are a significant determinant of household enrollments. On the other hand, per capita government expenditure on primary schools (a crude measure of school quality) has no significant impact on the likelihood of a child enrolling in primary school. So the quality of schools does not seem to influence enrollment decisions in this case. Direct costs (books, uniforms and transport) and household income also do not seem to affect enrollment significantly. However, the indirect or opportunity cost of children's time (particularly girls) is a significant determinant of enrollment. If opportunity costs are high in relation to household income and to expected future earnings, then households may forego schooling. Parents' education levels have a positive and significant impact on the probability of enrollment. The level of mothers' education exerts a particularly strong influence on the likelihood of girls enrolling in school. In addition, Mason and Khandker looked at environmental factors and found that the presence of electricity appears to have a positive impact on the probability of enrollment.

At secondary school level, the main findings are as follows. Household income significantly affects secondary enrollment decisions. Also, distances to secondary schools (public and private) play an important role in household schooling decisions. This means that monetary and time costs associated with travel to schools significantly affect secondary enrollment decisions. Also, the opportunity cost of girls' time has a significant influence on the probability of enrollment. On the other hand, direct costs of schooling appear to have no significant influence upon the probability of enrollment. Finally, the number of adults in the household (who can substitute for child labor) is a significant determinant of secondary school enrollment. The more adults there are in the household who can work, the more likely it is that children are free from labor and can attend school.

In addition, Mason and Khandker simulated the impact of two policy interventions on the transition rate from primary to secondary school. The first of these interventions was compensating households for the direct and indirect costs of secondary schools either through: (i) compensating households for school fees, contributions and school supplies, (ii) compensating households for the value of the opportunity cost of their children's time, and (iii) compensating households for both school fees, contributions and school supplies, and the opportunity costs of their children's time. The second intervention was: reducing distances to secondary schools to (i) 15 kilometers, (ii) 10 kilometers; and (iii) 5 kilometers.

They found that only modest improvements in secondary enrollments could be achieved through these two interventions, either individually or in combination. If households are compensated for the costs they incur, and the distance to school is reduced to no more than 10 kilometers, the impact on secondary enrollment increases is larger/significant. However, even in this case, the increase was still modest. Mason and Khandker note, however, that the results must be qualified by the fact that the supply of education at secondary was, until very recently, severely limited as a matter of policy.

A summary discussion

The above studies suggest that a significant number of variables or factors affect schooling decisions. These variables can be grouped in a number of ways. In addition to access and quality, the variables that affect demand for education are: direct costs, opportunity costs, benefits, availability of funds for schooling, and intra-household bargaining. The influence or weight that these variables have on household schooling decisions in the three studies can be summarized as follows.

(i) *Direct costs.* The evidence here is mixed, but there is a general sense from the three studies that at primary-level school, direct costs have only a minor influence upon the probability of enrollment in the two countries. This finding should be qualified. First, there are several countries in the region that charge substantial fees for primary school e.g. Uganda, Kenya. The impact of direct cost is likely to be significant in these countries. Second, evidence from Malawi, Zimbabwe and Ethiopia suggest that demand for primary schooling is price-elastic. Enrollments increased substantially after primary school fees were lowered or dropped in these countries. Furthermore, direct costs matter more for the poor than the rich. As the poor usually have more children, even nominal fees add up and exert a greater burden on their limited budgets.

(ii) *Opportunity costs.*[18] It is quite clear that the opportunity costs of children's (particularly girls) time is a significant determinant of enrollment. This remains true for a variety of proxies for opportunity costs: the occupation of the household; child wages; the distance of the household from its fuel wood source; distance to the household drinking water and the number of adults in the household (who can substitute for child labor).

(iii) *Benefits.* This determinant of household demand for education is not very well-studied in Africa. One of the reasons is that monetary benefits to primary education are hard to measure. It would be easier to demonstrate that future earnings is a significant determinant of enrollments at post-primary level. There is anecdotal evidence from several reports that suggests that parents find that schooling no longer yields the same rewards. For instance, primary and secondary school graduates are no longer guaranteed employment in the civil service. This used to represent a significant potential benefit for primary schooling. Also, with the decline in formal sector employment and the growth of informal sector work, several reports suggest that parents feel that for the kind of jobs

---

[18] See Annex for a discussion of the case of Madagascar.

available in the informal sector, education is not so important. Moreover, the present value of expected earnings from informal sector employment is low and does not always outweigh the cost of schooling.

(iv) *Availability of funds/credit market imperfection.* There is clear evidence that the level of economic welfare of the household increases enrollment probabilities. The size of this effect, however, varies across countries, regions (urban/rural) and levels of education (primary/secondary). The fact that income matters often means that the occupation of the head of household is a significant determinant of schooling choices (cash crop producers benefiting from guaranteed prices for their produce and wage earners - civil servants in particular - invest more in the education of their children). In all these cases, income matters because low-income households do not have access to credit markets and cannot borrow to meet the up-front costs of education. This suggests that another potential policy lever could be correcting credit market imperfections so that poor households can borrow to invest in education and repay later when the investment starts paying off. It also suggests that targeted scholarships as used in, for instance, Tanzania for secondary school enrollment for girls from poor households may be an effective instrument to promote enrollments.

(v) *Access/infrastructure.* The picture is again varied. Constraints in the supply of primary schools are a significant determinant of household enrollment. At the same time, per capita government expenditure on primary schools does not seem to have a significant impact on the likelihood of a child enrolling in primary school. Differences in educational attainment between regions of a same country may also reflect infrastructure disparities, such as the presence of electricity.

(vi) *Intra-household bargaining.* The sex of the head of household matters - a male head tends to favors boys' education more than a female head does. Female-headed households generally invest more in the education of the children. Also, parents' education level has a positive and significant impact on the probability of enrollment.

4. ARE THERE BETTER DIAGNOSTIC INSTRUMENTS?

Declining enrollment rates is a common problem in the region and one that cannot be left unattended. The region's educational attainment levels are the lowest in the world and the region needs the social as well as the economic benefits of education to improve institutions, and accelerate growth. The foregoing review of the literature has argued that the problem cannot simply be addressed by expanding access to schools and improving school quality. The studies reviewed above suggest that a more thorough investigation of the reasons for the declining demand for education is necessary. We need to know why households are reluctant to send their children to school. In order to better tailor policy responses, we need to investigate whether the same underlying reasons hold for urban or rural households, rich or poor households, girls or boys.

The studies show that it is not easy to assess the determinants of household demand. It is determined by many factors including the availability and quality of the schools. But households also take costs, and to a lesser extent potential benefits, into account. Constraints in access and poor-quality schools combined with relative high costs and low benefits almost certainly result in households not enrolling their children. But even by themselves, high costs and low benefits may be decisive constraints to enrollment or reasons for dropping out.

Efforts and investments to increase enrollment in the region should therefore be preceded by an analysis of demand as well as supply. The analysis of demand may not be necessary for every new investment or project in every country, but in cases where enrollments have declined and continue to do so despite adequate supply of school places, it would seem essential to analyze demand issues.

However, we do not have a simple instrument to assess demand in a manner that would provide information about variations, changes or problems in a particular country. Since we have seen that demand is likely to vary by locality or region, by income, or by gender, we would need an instrument that would capture the variations according to these criteria. Only after diagnosing the reasons for demand constraints will it be possible to decide on appropriate policies to remedy that situation.

The regression analyses discussed above for Côte d'Ivoire and Tanzania are probably the best way to diagnose demand. However, they are very data-intensive. A second-best analysis demanding less comprehensive data can be used to diagnose demand for education. We would like to suggest that a simple **private** rates of return (ROR) analysis done for different regions, income and gender groups for a specific country will provide meaningful information on education demand. The use of rates of return analysis in education has been a topic of debate in the sector. The debate has much intensified in recent years since the Bank decided to require an economic analysis for investments in education and training. We would like to refer briefly to some of the issues surrounding the use of ROR analysis and show that the way in which we propose to make use of it avoids the usual pitfalls and serves the purpose of identifying the reasons for differential demand for education among households of different types.

The traditional use of rates of return analysis

The Bank recommends the use of **social** rates of return to determine whether a project is desirable, and to rank investment priorities in the education sector. Computations of social rates of return, following Psacharopoulos (1973), have led to a series of now popular findings and recommendations for Sub-Saharan Africa: (i) ROR for all levels of education exceed the aggregate social opportunity cost of capital; (ii) ROR in developing countries (and especially Africa) are higher than in the advanced market economies; (iii) the pattern of ROR remains stable as countries develop with only relatively minor declines in ROR. These findings imply that education at whatever level is a relatively attractive investment for individuals and for governments.

Table 2: Return to Investment in Education by Level (%), Regional Averages

	Social			Private		
	Primary	Secondary	Higher	Primary	Secondary	Higher
SSA	24.3	18.2	11.2	41.3	26.6	27.8
OECD	14.4	10.2	8.7	21.7	12.4	12.3

Source: Psacharopoulos (1994)

These optimistic findings, however, seemed to be contradicted by the fact that enrollments have stagnated - why should enrollments be on the decline if education is such an attractive investment?[19] The disconnect between the predictions from the rates of return literature and the actual behavior of households[20] has led to discussions about the methods of calculating ROR and suggestions for improving the methodology.

(i) *Alternative methods of calculations*. A number of authors resolved the apparent contradiction simply by using a much more thorough analysis of the costs and benefits associated with education. Mason and Khandker, in the study discussed above, carried out an investigation of rates of return to primary and secondary education in Tanzania.[21] Their analysis showed that rates of return were low by regional standards, and that they may have declined from the levels reported in the 1980s. The private incentives for Tanzanian households to invest in education therefore did not appear to be particularly

---

[19] There are two ways - of some relevance - of solving the contradiction: (i) there is an information problem and households are not aware of the potentially very large benefits of education; (ii) households perceive that returns from education are high but cannot invest because of budget constraints and inability to borrow on credit markets.

[20] Estimated rates of return to investment in schooling in developing countries tend to be higher for girls than for boys - which is again hard to reconcile with the revealed choices of households.

[21] Using hourly earnings in the formal wage sector as a measure of benefits, they find private rates to education to be 7.9 percent at the primary level and 8.8 percent at the secondary level.

strong. The substantial decline in enrollment rates mentioned earlier would therefore not be surprising.

(ii) *The aggregation problem.* Bennell (1994) is critical of the aggregation of rates of return from country studies into region-wide rates of return. He finds that in the Africa region: (i) social ROR for all levels of education have fallen significantly during the last two decades (with wage employment opportunities remaining minimal). In a growing number of SSA countries, social ROR may now be lower than the aggregate social opportunity cost of capital; (ii) with chronically low internal and external efficiencies at all education levels in most SSA countries, it seems highly implausible that ROR in SSA are higher than in the advanced industrial countries; (iii) the pattern of ROR in SSA is unstable with the available evidence showing major declines in ROR as countries have been rocked by economic, political and social crises.

(iii) *Average versus marginal rates of return.* Knight and Sabot (1992) argue that what is usually measured in rate of return studies is the *average* return to education. However, from the human capital theory point of view, the *marginal* returns should be used. In the majority of the studies, the assumption is made that the average wage of labor measures the wage received by the marginal (i.e. most recently recruited) worker. The performance in the labor market of *all* those completing primary school is thus used in these studies to estimate the expected earnings stream of recent primary school completers. However, labor market conditions faced by new entrants tend to be dramatically different for many reasons, including the fact that expansion of education enrollment has led to a consequent increase in the supply of educated workers. It is likely that the performance of primary completers who left school ten or twenty years earlier will be a bad predictor for those entering the labor market today. The practice of using average instead of marginal returns is probably one of the reasons for the overestimations of returns to education in the region.

(iv) *The expectations dimension of schooling.* Rates of return calculations could also be improved if the expected average number of years it takes to complete school were taken into account in estimating opportunity costs rather than the standard or formal duration of schooling. Given the low internal efficiency of education in many African countries, the actual number of years it takes to graduate is far higher than the formal one.[22] Ignoring the expectations dimensions can lead to estimations of opportunity costs that are *four or five times lower* than they actually are. Using the expected average duration rather than the formal one would reduce the rates of return dramatically since opportunity costs usually constitute the bulk of private costs.[23] Rates of return estimates could also be improved by taking seriously the expectations concerning benefits. Expected benefits are based upon labor market perceptions, i.e. not only upon expected incremental wages upon graduation, but also on employment opportunities. In a number of countries, those who

---

[22] In the Comoros, it takes 29.6 student-years to produce one primary school graduate (see SAR, Third Education Project, Comoros, May 1997).

[23] See Mason and Khandker on Tanzania (1996).

completed school, especially secondary school, were almost guaranteed employment in the civil service. This expectation in terms of employment was often the driving force behind household demand for education. In those countries, the freeze in civil service employment that accompanied structural adjustment programs may have caused the expected benefits to education to plummet. Rates of return calculations would capture this change only insofar as they factor in employment opportunities as well as incremental wages.

(v) *Externalities.* Another criticism[24] of the prevailing rates of return is that they do not calculate what they propose to do - namely **social** rates of return. Social rates differ from private rates in that they include those cost and benefits that accrue to society over and above those captured by the households. While the rates of return calculations in the literature do a good job of capturing social costs, they do not capture social benefits - or positive externalities - associated with education investments. The failure to compute the social benefits to education is due to the difficulties to identify and value the externalities associated with education (effects on co-worker productivity, on fertility, on health, on civil order, etc.). Summers (1992) and Mingat and Tan (1996) provide two innovative and relatively isolated attempts at valuing externalities. Social rates of return that do not include social benefits cannot properly inform policy decisions. The rationale for public intervention in education should ideally be based on the fact that households' investment in education may be sub-optimal since they do not take into account the benefits that accrue to the society. Therefore, since the rates of return of investments are exclusive of externalities, they may mislead policymakers as to what the priority investments for public sector are. A particular sub-sector for which rates of return *exclusive of externalities* are high may not warrant priority public sector investment. One could also argue that public sector investments could be crowding out private investment in a lucrative sector.

Using rates of return analysis to assess demand for education

The use that we propose of rates of return, avoids the majority of the above pitfalls, while helping to inform policy makers about the demand for education so that policy responses are more focused. What we advocate is to assess the relative demand for education between different localities or between urban and rural areas, between households with different levels of income, and by gender. This can be done, depending on data availability, by creating a table with the following data: enrollment rates for boys and girls (colums 1 and 2); average income (column 3); opportunity costs for boys and girls (columns 4 and 5); direct costs for boys and girls (colums 6 and 7); estimated benefits for boys and girls (colums 8 and 9); and estimated private rate of return for boys and girls (colums 10 and 11). These elements would be computed for each region or geographic sub-division that makes sense or for which data are available.

---

[24] See Hammer (1996).

Table 3: Private Rates of Return by Region

	Enrollment rates		Average income	Opport. costs		Direct costs		Private benefits		Private ROR	
	Boys	Girls		Boys	Girls	Boys	Girls	Boys	Girls	Boys	Girls
Region i											
Region j											
Region k											

Source: Authors (1997)

The analysis of the data in the table would provide useful information about education demand. The primary use would be to show that rates of return are likely to vary between different parts of a country, and according to the gender of the child. High private rates of return that go together with high enrollment rates would suggest that costs and benefits are no issue. Low rates of return on the other hand supported by data showing low or declining enrollments would suggest that households are not convinced that the present value of education benefits outweighs education costs. If the low rates of return are combined with high or above average direct or opportunity costs, this would suggest that the cost of education is the principal reason for withholding schooling. The policy implication could then be to design ways of reducing the cost of education for these households. There are many ways to do this - through subsidies, vouchers, cost reduction methods, or modifications in the school calendar. The feasibility of these measures will not be discussed here.

The table may also show that rates of return are low because expected benefits are low. Low expected benefits are more difficult to deal with in terms of education policies since these expectations are about employment opportunities and earnings. The latter are however largely determined by macroeconomic policies and much less by education sector ones. Low benefits may suggest that macroeconomic policies promoting growth are not in place. Maintaining sound macroeconomic policies is an important element in ensuring effective demand for education. Also, low expected benefits may be a result of lack of information by the household of the long-term benefits or the external benefits of schooling. It may also be an indication of poor quality of schooling. Additional information would be necessary to determine which one of these reasons is the more likely one. Each would require different policy responses.

One more observation. While few education investment projects include public information campaigns, the research shows that even in industrial countries, households make schooling decisions on the basis of estimated short-term or immediate benefits - for instance, the current income levels between different professions or graduates. Very few households seem to take life-long benefits into account. In developing countries where lack of information is chronic, households are likely to have much less information about long-term benefits. This lack of information is likely to reduce their demand for schooling. It would seem that governments need to pay more attention to public information about schooling. But also, donor-supported education investments should include public information campaign components.

Another interesting scenario would be the combination of high rates of return with low enrollments. In that event, it may be surmised that the constraining factor would be the household's limited access to credit or that access to school is constrained.

The table may help design region-specific policy responses according to the patterns of enrollment vis-à-vis private rates of return that they display.

The proposed use of the rates of return would avoid the major pitfall associated with computing social rates of return, which is omitting externalities. There is no theoretical need here to compute externalities and we do not encounter the computational problems associated with that. Some of the other pitfalls can also be avoided: (i) by using current labor market entry graduate salaries, rather than the performance in the labor market of all those completing a particular education cycle; and (ii) by paying attention to the expectations dimensions of opportunity costs and benefits. Aggregation is *de facto* not a problem in this particular use of rates of return.

This approach should help to diagnose which of the costs, benefits, or the economic condition of the household, are playing a role in the decline of enrollments in the region. If the diagnosis is confirmed that declining enrollments are not solely the product of schooling supply constraint, governments would have to devise a gamut of cost-reducing and demand stimulating programs, and not limit intervention to access and quality.

5. CONCLUSION

The decline of enrollments in the region must necessarily be reversed. The social and economic well-being of the people in the region will improve with more and better education. Interventions to check declines in enrollments should in most countries in the region not be restricted to improving school availability and quality. These two measures are necessary, but they may not be sufficient. We have argued that in addition to constraints in access and quality, households consider other costs and benefits of education in their schooling decisions. The cost of education in many countries is high in relation to incomes and the benefits have deteriorated with declining employment opportunities. We have suggested using a private rate of return analysis to assess if and how costs and benefits considerations play a role in declining enrollments. If households keep their children at home because they cannot afford to send them or because they consider education not worthwhile, then governments must come up with measures to address these issues. Where supply rationing is not the cause of declining enrollments, cost reduction and demand stimulation measures as well as public information campaigns to influence the way people think about benefits, are what could be attempted to reverse enrollment declines.

ANNEX: A CURSORY EXAMINATION OF PRIMARY SCHOOL ENROLLMENTS AND OPPORTUNITY COSTS IN MADAGASCAR FROM A GENDER PERSPECTIVE

Girls and boys enrollments in Madagascar: an atypical scenario

Girls' schooling in Madagascar does not follow the same pattern as most other African countries. Indeed, it would appear that there is no significant bias against the enrollment of girls in both primary and secondary schools.

Table 1a: Primary School Enrollment Data

Primary schooling	Sex	1990	1992
Number of students	Boys + Girls	1,570,721	1,490,317
	Girls	773,797	726,412
	Girls	49.3	48.7
Gross enrollment rate	Boys	89	77
	Girls	85	74
	Boys - Girls	4	3
Net enrollment rates	Boys	60	-
	Girls	59	-
	Boys - Girls	1	-
Apparent intake ratio	Boys	84	80
	Girls	87	79
	Boys - Girls	-3	1
Survival rate to CM1	Boys	21.9	25.6
	Girls	20.9	29.7
	Boys - Girls	1.0	-4.1
Efficiency coefficient	Boys	27	31
	Girls	28	35
	Boys - Girls	-1	-4

Source: UNESCO (1995)

Table 1b: Secondary School Enrollment Data

Secondary schooling	Sex	1990	1992
Gross enrollment rate	Boys	17	15
	Girls	17	15
	Boys - Girls	0	0
Primary to general secondary	Boys	43.8	35.0
Transition rate	Girls	41.4	34.7
	Boys - Girls	2.4	0.3

Source: UNESCO (1995)

The claim that there is no systematic bias in Madagascar against girl's education therefore seems to be valid for a whole gamut of indicators. Girls get enrolled and stay in the school system at roughly the same rate as boys do.

The data base for Madagascar being rather poor, we thought it appropriate to check whether the 1996 household survey data conveys information that is consistent with the above findings. We looked at the gross and net enrollment rates by sex, region and income level computed from the survey data. The findings are summarized in the table below.[25]

---

[25] See Madagascar Poverty Assessment (1996), vol.2 , page 149, Annex Table D-3.

Table 2: Gross and Net Enrollment Rates

	Gross enrollment rates				Net enrollment rates			
	Primary		Secondary		Primary		Secondary	
Quintile	Boys	Girls	Boys	Girls	Boys	Girls	Boys	Girls
1	50	49	2	3	29	28	0	1
Rural	48	46	2	2	28	26	0	1
Urban	99	100	9	9	54	56	1	1
2	85	81	9	8	45	47	3	3
Rural	81	79	8	6	42	44	2	3
Urban	124	106	20	21	70	72	7	4
3	85	86	10	9	47	51	3	4
Rural	80	83	7	7	45	49	2	4
Urban	129	105	29	22	64	64	9	9
4	97	104	25	24	54	59	8	10
Rural	85	96	15	14	48	54	6	5
Urban	142	133	53	52	76	77	14	22
5	102	114	48	42	62	70	18	22
Rural	78	101	23	21	50	60	8	13
Urban	151	138	85	75	86	90	32	35
Total	81	84	19	18	46	50	6	8
Rural	72	77	10	9	41	44	3	5
Urban	137	124	56	52	75	79	19	23

Source: Authors (1997)

The data above do not exactly tally with the data from Tables 1a and 1b. However, it is again clear that gender bias is not significant. If anything, one may even point to a bias against boys' education. In urban areas, while the gross rates indicate a higher male participation (137 against 124 for girls), the net rates indicate the opposite bias (75 for boys and 79 for girls). In rural areas, both gross and net rates indicate a higher female participation in the school system.

Primary schooling and opportunity costs linked to household chores

Human capital theory proposes a model of schooling-choice that is based upon a cost-benefit calculation. The household chooses to send its offspring to school because the education costs present are more than matched by the discounted value of future benefits. Costs are of two kinds: direct costs which include such items as school fees, transportation to school, uniforms, learning materials; and opportunity costs, or the earnings relinquished by the household because the child is not engaged in an income-earning activity all the time he/she is at school. Benefits come in the shape of the higher future earnings typically associated with higher education levels.

One can conveniently group the variables that affect education costs and benefits (and, by extension, schooling choices) into four categories: (i) individual characteristics (age, sex, relationship with head of household); (ii) household characteristics (household income, size of household, education level of parents); (iii) school characteristics (school fees, distance from school, rationing of places); and (iv) regional or national characteristics (distance from water source, presence of electricity, regional opportunity costs of schooling, regional labor market participation rates, expected earnings by education level).

One can start tracing potential sources for gender biases from these parameters of costs and benefits. If boys and girls are engaged in different activities in the household, then their opportunity costs are likely to be different. Everything else being the same, the household might be led to make gender-specific schooling choices. The same applies for benefits: if there is a significant difference between potential earnings for boys and girls of similar education levels, then, other things being equal, there is an incentive for households to focus on the schooling of children of one particular gender. Gender differences are likely to be less significant as far as direct costs are concerned - transportation costs, school fees, uniform costs, learning materials are equally expensive for boys and girls.[26]

In this section, we focus on various components of the opportunity costs of primary school boys and girls in Madagascar. We use time-allocation data as a manner of approximating opportunity costs. In the econometric literature on household demand for education, opportunity costs loom large as an inhibiting factor to schooling. In addition, there is the widespread belief that opportunity costs (more than direct costs or benefits) are the main factor driving gender biases in schooling. We do not investigate here the relative weight of opportunity costs in the household's schooling choices because that would involve a full-blown demand analysis. Instead, we discuss whether opportunity costs (as approximated by time-allocation data) for boys and girls in Madagascar are consistent with the fact that girls and boys attend school in much the same fashion in Madagascar.

a.   Water collection

The following table summarizes the degree of participation of children of (primary) school-going age by gender and by schooling status for in water-collection.

---

[26] The average annual direct schooling costs were about 20,000 FMG (US$ .3.64) for both boys and girls (computed from survey data).

Table 3a: School Participation Rates
(percent)

	Children of school-going age who			
	do not go to school		go to school	
	Boys	Girls	Boys	Girls
Spent time collecting water	37	83	41	58
Did not spend time collecting water	63	17	59	42
Total	100	100	100	100

Source: Authors (1997)

From the table above, girls seem to be more consistently involved in the water-collecting activity whether or not they go to school. Boys are also involved in this activity, although to a lesser extent than girls. It is also interesting to note that girls relinquish water-collecting when they go to school to a much greater extent than boys do. The table below shows the average number of hours spent weekly collecting water by boys and girls and seems to confirm the above findings.

Table 3b: Average Hours Spent Collecting Water

	Children of school-going age who			
	do not go to school		go to school	
	Boys	Girls	Boys	Girls
Average number of hours spent collecting water per week	1.4	4.1	1.5	2.3

Source: Authors (1997)

Again it appears that (i) boys are less heavily involved in this type of activity regardless of whether they go to school or not; (ii) girls are heavily involved in that activity; (iii) girls who attend school relinquish the activity to a great extent, although they are even then still more involved in it than boys are.

b. Firewood collection

Children are involved in a number of other gender-specific household tasks. Firewood collection is generally taken to be a primarily male activity. The tables below confirm that this is the case for Malgache children as well.

Table 4a: School Participation in Relation to Collection Firewood (percent)

| | Children of school-going age who | | | |
| | do not go to school | | go to school | |
	Boys	Girls	Boys	Girls
Spent time collecting firewood	54	20	23	11
Did not spend time collecting firewood	46	80	77	89
Total	100	100	100	100

Source: Authors (1997)

Table 4b: School Participation and Time Spent Collecting Firewood

| | Children of school-going age who | | | |
| | do not go to school | | go to school | |
	Boys	Girls	Boys	Girls
Average number of hours spent fetching firewood per week	3.0	1.0	1.1	0.5

Source: Authors (1997)

Boys obviously spend much more time on average than girls fetching firewood. They also relinquish proportionally more of this activity when they go to school. But even when they do go to school, they are still more heavily involved in this activity than girls. The situation here is the mirror image of water-collection in terms of gender involvement.

c.   Other household tasks

These include the preparation of meals, running errands, house-cleaning and maintenance, child-minding and rearing). We again check for eventual differences in the degree of participation by gender in these activities

Table 5a: School Participation and Time Spent on Household Tasks (per cent)

| | Children of school-going age who | | | |
| | do not go to school | | go to school | |
	Boys	Girls	Boys	Girls
Spent time on other household tasks	42	87	37	60
Did not spend time on other household tasks	58	13	63	40
Total	100	100	100	100

Source: Authors (1997)

Table 5b: School Participation and Time Spent on Household Tasks

| | Children of school-going age who | | | |
| | do not go to school | | go to school | |
	Boys	Girls	Boys	Girls
Average number of hours spent on other household tasks per week	4.5	16.0	3.0	6.0

Source: Authors (1997)

Once again, girls are much more involved in these household tasks than boys are, regardless whether they go to school or not. Girls "give up" on average 10 hours per week of these tasks when they go to school; boys give up a mere 1.5 hours.

The table below adds up the number of hours spent by girls and boys in all the household tasks (i.e. water-collection + firewood collection + other tasks).

Table 5c: School Participation and Time Spent on All Tasks

| | Children of school-going age who | | | |
| | do not go to school | | go to school | |
	Boys	Girls	Boys	Girls
Average number of hours spent on **all** household tasks per week	8.9	21.1	5.6	8.8

Source: Authors (1997)

An unsophisticated reading of the table could be as follows: household tasks are primarily done by girls, and sending a girl to school has a "cost" of (21.1 - 8.8 =) 12.3 hours of work, while sending a boy to school only "costs" (8.9 - 5.6 =) 3.3 hours of work. If this were the sum of activities of children, then we would expect households to favor the schooling of boys. However, children are also engaged in "independent" (and sometimes income-earning) activities where boys' participation is likely to be more significant. If that were to be the case, then the total opportunity costs of boys' schooling could be similar to that of girls.

Primary schooling and opportunity costs linked to independent agricultural and non-agricultural activities

The table below shows the proportion of children of primary school-going age engaged in paid employment (over the 12 months prior to the survey).

Table 6a: School Participation and Employment
(per cent)

	Children of school-going age who			
	do not go to school		go to school	
	Boys	Girls	Boys	Girls
Was involved in paid employment over the past 12 months	9.2	13.1	1.2	0.6
Wasn't involved in paid employment	90.8	86.9	98.8	99.4
Total	100	100	100	100

Source: Authors (1997)

The table indicates that children of school-going age are not very involved in paid employment even when they do not attend school; the participation rates for girls are marginally higher than for boys.

The following tables compare the level of participation of boys and girls in independent agricultural and non-agricultural activities.

Table 6b: School Participation in Relation to Non-Agricultural Activities
(percent)

	Children of school-going age who			
	do not go to school		go to school	
	Boys	Girls	Boys	Girls
Was involved in an independent non-agricultural activity over past 12 months	0.8	3.6	0.1	0.1
Not involved in such an activity	99.2	96.4	99.9	99.9

Source: Authors (1997)

Participation rates in non-agricultural activities are very low for both sexes - albeit slightly higher for girls who do not attend primary school.

**Table 6c: School Participation in Relation to Agricultural Activities
(percent)**

| | Children of school-going age who | | | |
| | do not go to school | | go to school | |
	Boys	Girls	Boys	Girls
Was involved in an independent agricultural activity over past 12 months	63.6	56.0	15.3	12.9
Was not involved in such an activity	36.4	44.0	84.7	87.1
Total	100	100	100	100

Source: Authors (1997)

The case is very different for agricultural activities - here the participation rates are very high for both sexes, with boys being marginally more active.

The actual workload for boys and girls in these independent activities is not given by the tables above so that it is not possible yet to establish what the typical weekly workload is. The following table focuses on the time spent on the principal independent occupation - the secondary and tertiary occupations are marginal for this age-group.

Table 6d: School Participation and Time Spent in Principal Occupation

| | Children of school-going age who | | | |
| | do not go to school | | go to school | |
	Boys	Girls	Boys	Girls
Number of weeks over past 12 months spent working in principal occupation	44.4	42.7	37.7	32.9
Number of days per weeks usually spent working in principal occupation	5.6	5.4	4.9	4.5
Number of hours per day usually spent working in principal occupation	6.3	5.5	3.8	3.5

Source: Authors (1997)

The table shows that boys more than girls are employed in independent activities - on average, a boy attending school works 183.4 more hours than a girl attending school per year; a boy not attending school works 298.2 hours more than his female counterpart. In addition, the household relinquishes 864 hours of work a year when the boy goes to school as against 750 hours when the girl does so. While, therefore, the opportunity cost of girls' schooling proved to be higher than that of boys' because of their higher involvement in household tasks, that of boys is higher because of their higher participation rate in independent activities.

Primary schooling and opportunity costs: a concluding summary

The table below synthesizes the information discussed above:

Table 7a: School Participation in Relation to Specific Tasks

| (hrs per week) | Children of school-going age who are | | | |
| | not at school (hours) | | at school (hours) | |
	Boys	Girls	Boys	Girls
Water collection	1.4	4.1	1.5	2.3
Wood collection	3.0	1.0	1.1	0.5
Other household tasks	4.5	16.0	3.0	6.0
Total household tasks	8.9	21.1	5.6	8.8
Principal occupation	35.3	29.7	18.6	15.8
Total non-school activities	44.2	50.8	24.2	24.6

Source: Authors (1997)

If we were to value the contribution of children to households in simplistic terms of hours worked, then the table above shows that the opportunity cost of girls' schooling is an average of (50.8 - 24.6 =) 26.2 hours and that of boys is (44.2 - 24.2 =) 20.0 hours per week. The table below shows this with further disaggregation:

Table 7b: Hours Worked by Tasks

| | Opportunity Costs (hours) | |
	Boys	Girls
Household activities	3.3	12.3
Principal independent activity	16.7	13.9
Total non-school activities	20.0	26.2

Source: Authors (1997)

Raw time-allocation data therefore indicates that girls contribute more labor to the households than boys do - one would therefore expect, other things being equal, that parents would be more reluctant to send their girls to school. The direct comparison between hours worked by boys and girls is however not appropriate since (i) boys are engaged in an independent activity over a much longer period of time during the year, and (ii) the principal occupation is valued differently for boys and girls. Adjusting the number of hours girls work in the principal occupation for these two elements,[27] we obtain 9.3 hours instead of the 13.9 hours in the unadjusted case. Therefore, the adjusted

---

[27] Adjusted hours = unadjusted hours x (weeks girls per year spend on main occupation/ weeks per year boys spend in main occupation) x (average wage of girls in principal occupation/ average wage of boys in principal occupation). Here we used agricultural wages for boys and girls to approximate their relative earnings in the principal occupation. 9.3 = 13.9 x (32.9/37.7) x 0.77.

number of hours girls spend on non-school activities is (12.3 + 9.3 =) 21.6 hours, which is not significantly different from the number of hours boys work. The pattern of opportunity costs therefore seems to be entirely consistent with the pattern of identical enrollments in primary schools.

From a pure theoretically point of view, this is a very one-sided approach to the question of determinants of schooling-choices because we say nothing of the expected benefits from education. In order to make a robust statement as to the fact that girls and boys' enrollments in Madagascar are identical because the opportunity costs households incur are similar in both cases, we would also need to demonstrate that expected benefits by level of education are equivalent for boys and girls. However, opportunity costs are a much more important determinant of schooling choices than future earnings at *primary school level*. Thus, the analysis carried out above probably captures the fundamentals of the enrollment pattern.

Adams A.V., R. Goldfarb and T. Kelly. "How the Macroeconomic Environment Affects Human Resource Development." Working Paper 828. World Bank. Washington, DC. 1992.

Adams, J.D. "The Threat to Education from Structural Adjustment: A Realistic Response." IDS Bulletin, 20: 1 January 1989.

Appleton S. *Socio-economic Determinants of Education, Health and Fertility in Africa.* D. Phil Thesis. Oxford. 1991.

Appleton, S., P. Collier and P. Horsnell. "Gender: Education and Employment in Côte d'Ivoire." SDA Working Paper 8. World Bank. Washington, DC. 1990.

Barr, N.A. *The Economics of the Welfare State.* London: Weidenfeld and Nicolson.. 1993.

Barro, R. "Government Spending in a Simple Model of Endogenous Growth," *Journal of Political Economy*, 98: S103-S125. 1990.

Barro R. J. "Economic Growth in a Cross-Section of Countries." *Quarterly Journal of Economics.* Vol. 106, Iss. 2. May 1991.

_____and J-W. Lee. "International Comparisons of Educational Attainment," paper present at the World Bank conference "How do National Policies Affect Long-Run Growth?" Washington DC. February 1993.

Becker G.S. "Investment in human capital: a theoretical analysis," *Journal of Political Economy*, 70, I (5): 9-49. 1962.

_____. *Human Capital: A Theoretical and Empirical Analysis, with Special Reference to Education:* Columbia University Press. 1975.

Becker, G., K.M. Murphy and R. Tamura "Human Capital, Fertility and Economic Growth," *Journal of Political Economy*, 98: S12-S37. 1990.

Behrman J. "Analysing Human Resources Effects: Education,*"Understanding the Social Effects of Policy Reforms."* Washington, DC: World Bank. 1993.

Bennell, P. "Rates of Return to Education: Does the conventional pattern prevail in Sub-Saharan Africa?" Institute of Development Studies. Sussex. 1994.

_____. "Rates of Return in Asia: A Review of the Evidence." Institute of Development Studies. Sussex. September 1995.

Birdsall, N. "Public Inputs and Child Schooling in Brazil," *Journal of Development Economics*. 18: 67-86. 1985.

Bouton, L., C. Jones and M. Kiguel. *Macroeconomic Reform and Growth in Africa. Policy Research Working Paper 1394*. World Bank. Washington, D.C. 1994.

Collier, P., A. C. Edwards, J. Roberts and K. Bardhan. "Gender aspects of labour market allocation during structural adjustment" in S. Horton, R. Kanbur, and D. Mazumdar, eds. *Labour Markets in an Era of Adjustment.* EDI Development Studies. World Bank. 1994.

Demery, L. "Analyzing the Mesoeconomic Effects of Structural Adjustment," Chapter 2 in *Understanding the Social Effects of Policy Reform.* World Bank. Washington, DC. 1993.

Devarajan S., L. Squire, and S. Suthiwart-Narueput. *"Beyond Rates of Return: Reorienting Project Appraisal."* Policy Research Department. World Bank. Washington, DC. January 1996.

De Vreyer, P. 'Une analyse économétrique de la demande d'éducation en Côte d'Ivoire," *Revue d'Economie du Développement*, No. 3. September1993.

Fisher, S. "Macroeconomic Factors in Growth," in How do National Policies Affect Long-Run Growth? Conference at the World Bank. Washington, DC. February 1993.

Freeman, R.B. "Demand Elasticities for Educated Labour" in G. Psacharopoulos, ed. *Economics of Education: Research and Studies.* Pergamon Press. 1987.

_____. "Supply Elasticities for Educated Labour" in G. Psacharopoulos, ed. *Economics of Education: Research and Studies.* Pergamon Press. 1987.

_____. *"Demand for Education,"* O. Ashenfelter, R. Layard, eds. Chapter 6. Handbook of Labour Economics. Volume 1. 1986.

Griffin P., and A. Cox Edwards. "Rates of Return to Education in Brazil: Do Labour Market Conditions Matter?" *Economics of Education Review.* 12 (3): 245-255. 1993.

Griliches, Z. "Notes on the role of education in production functions and growth accounting" in W.L. Hansen, ed. Education, Income and Human Capital. *Studies in Income and Wealth*, 35: pp. 71-115, NBER. 1970.

Hammer, J. "Memorandum to PRDPE." World Bank. Washington, DC. January 22, 1996.

Hanushek, E.A. "Interpreting recent research on schooling in developing countries," *World Bank Research Observer*, 10 (2). August 1995.

Heneveld, W. "Planning and Monitoring the Quality of Primary Education in SSA." AFTHR Note 14. World Bank. Washington, DC. 1994.

Hicks, N.L. "Education and Economic Growth" in G. Psacharopoulos, ed. *Economics of Education: Research and Studies.* Pergamon Press. 1987.

Hinchliffe K. "Education and the Labour Market" in G. Psacharopoulos, ed. *Economics of Education: Research and Studies.* Pergamon Press. 1987.

_____. "Public Sector Employment and Education" in G. Psacharopoulos, ed. *Economics of Education: Research and Studies.* Pergamon Press. 1987.

Jamison, D.T., and L. L. Lau. *Farmer Education and Farm Efficienc.* Johns Hopkins University Press. 1982.

Kakwani, N., E. Makonnen, and J. van der Gaag. *"Structural Adjustment and Living Conditions in Developing Countries."* PRE Working Paper. No. WPS 467. World Bank, Washington, DC. August 1990.

Kelly, M.J. "Education in a Declining Economy - The Case of Zambia 1975-1985." EDI. World Bank. Washington, DC. 1991.

King, E. M. "Does the Price of Schooling Matter? Fees. Opportunity Costs, and Enrollments in Indonesia." PHRD. World Bank, Washington, DC. 1995.

Lilliard L.A. "Models for Analysing Schooling Choices with Household Survey Data." The Rand Corporation. N-1963-AID. 1984.

Knight, J.B. and, R. H. Sabot. "Education, Productivity and Inequality - The East African Natural Experiment," *Research Publication*. World Bank. 1990.

_____ and D.C., Hovey. Is the Rate of Return on Primary Schooling Really 26 percent? *Journal of African Economies.* 1 (2). August 1992.

_____. "The Rate of Return and Educational Expansion," *Economics of Education Review.* 6. (3): 255-262. 1987.

Lavy, V. *"Investment in Human Capital, Schooling Supply Constraints in Rural Ghana,"* LSMS Working Paper No. 93. World Bank. Washington, DC. 1992.

Layard, R., and G. Psacharopoulos. "The Screening Hypothesis and the Returns to Education," *Journal of Political Economy.* 82:. 985-98. 1970.

Lucas, R.E. "On the Mechanics of Economic Development," *Journal of Monetary Economics*. 22: 3-42. 1988.

Mason, A., and S.R. Khandker. *Household Schooling Decisions in Tanzania*. PSP. World Bank. Washington, DC. 1996.

McMahon, W.W. "Consumption and Other Benefits of Education" in G. Psacharopoulos, ed. *Economics of Education: Research and Studies*. Pergamon Press,. 1987.

_____. "Expected Rates of Return to Education" in G. Psacharopoulos, ed. *Economics of Education: Research and Studies*. Pergamon Press. 1987.

_____. "Student Labour Market Expectations" in G. Psacharopoulos, ed. *Economics of Education: Research and Studies*. Pergamon Press. 1987.

McNabb, R. "Labour Market Theories and Education" in G. Psacharopoulos, ed. *Economics of Education: Research and Studies*. Pergamon Press. 1987.

Mingat. A., and J.P. Tan. *"The Full Social Returns to Education: Estimates Based on Countries' Economic Growth Performance."* HCD Working Paper No. 73. September 1996.

Noss, A.. *"Education and Adjustment, A Review of the Literature,"* WPS 701. World Bank. Washington, DC. June 1991.

Palme, M.. "The Meaning of School Repetition and Dropout in the Mozambican Primary School." Department of Educational Research. Stockholm Institute of Education. 1993.

Paredes, R., and L.A. Riveros, eds. *"Human Resources and the Adjustment Process."* IDB. 1994.

Pritchett, L.. "Where has all the education gone?" World Bank. Washington, DC. June 1995.

Psacharopoulos, G. "Time Trends of the Returns to Education": Cross-National Evidence. *Economics of Education Review*. 8 (3): 225-231. 1989.

_____. "Returns to Investment in Education A Global Update," *World Development*. 22 (9): 1325-1344. 1994.

Ribe, H., and S. Carvalho. *"World Bank Treatment of the Social Impact of Adjustment Programs."* PRE Working Paper No. 521. World Bank. Washington, DC. 1990.

Romer, P.M.. "Increasing Returns and Long-Run Growth," *Journal of Political Economy*. 94 (5). 1986.

_____. "Human Capital and Growth: Theory and Evidence," NBER Working Paper Series. No. 3173. November 1989.

_____. Endogenous Technical Change. *Journal of Political Economy*. 98: S71-S102. 1990.

Rosenzweig, M.R. "Population Growth and Human Capital Investments: Theory and Evidence," *Journal of Political Economy*. 98: pp S38-S70. 1990.

_____. "Why are there Returns to Schooling*?" American Economic Review. Papers and Proceedings*. 85 (2): pp 153-158. 1995.

Schultz, T.P. "Education Investments and Returns," Chenery H., Srinivasan T.N., eds. *Handbook of Development Economics*. University of Chicago Press. Chapter 13. Volume 1. 1988.

_____. *Investing in People - The Economics of Population Quality*. University of California Press. 1981.

_____. "The Economic Value of Education," Columbia University Press. 1963.

Sheng Cheng Hu. "Education and Economic Growth," *Review of Economic Studies*. 1975.

Shields, N.G. "Female Labor and Education" in G. Psacharopoulos, ed. *Economics of Education: Research and Studies*. Pergamon Press. 1987.

Solow, R. "Technical Change and the Aggregate Production Function," *Review of Economics and Statistics*. 39:. 312-320. 1957.

Summers L.H. *Investing in All the People*. Policy Research Papers. WPS 905. World Bank. Washington, DC. 1992.

TADREG. "Parent's Attitudes Towards Education in Rural Tanzania." Research Report No. 5. November 1993.

Taubman P. and T. Wales. *Higher Education and Earnings: College as an Investment and a Screening Device*. McGraw-Hill. New York. 1974.

Tilak, J.B.G. "Economic Slowdown and Education Recession in Latin America." IDS Bulletin, 20.(1). January 1989.

UNESCO. "Female Participation in Sub-Saharan Africa." African Academy of Sciences. 1995.

Wiseman, J. "Public Finance in Education" in G. Psacharopoulos, ed. *Economics of Education: Research and Studies*. Pergamon Press. 1987.

Wolpin, K.I. "Education and Screening," *American Economic Review*. 67: 949-58. 1977.

Woodhall, M. "Earnings and Education" in G. Psacharopoulos, ed.. *Economics of Education: Research and Studies*. Pergamon Press. 1987.

World Bank. *Adjustment in Africa*. 1994.

_____. *Madagascar Poverty Assessment*. Report No. 14044-MAG. June 28, 1996.

_____. *Priorities and Strategies For Education - A World Bank Sector Review*. ESP. March 1995.

_____. Regional Perspectives on "WDR 1995. Improving Labour Market Outcomes in SSA," Draft. May 1995.

_____. *Project Appraisal Document on a Proposed ITF to Burkina Faso for a Post-Primary Education Project*. Report No. 16025-BUR. November 1996.

_____. *Staff Appraisal Report for a Third Education Project in the Islamic Federal Republic of the Comoros*. Report No. 16735-COM. May 1997.

Distributors of World Bank Publications

Prices and credit terms vary from country to country. Consult your local distributor before placing an order.

ARGENTINA
Oficina del Libro Internacional
Av. Córdoba 1877
1120 Buenos Aires
Tel: (54 1) 815-8354
Fax: (54 1) 815-8156
E-mail: olilibro@satlink.com

AUSTRALIA, FIJI, PAPUA NEW GUINEA, SOLOMON ISLANDS, VANUATU, AND SAMOA
D.A. Information Services
648 Whitehorse Road
Mitcham 3132
Victoria
Tel: (61) 3 9210 7777
Fax: (61) 3 9210 7788
E-mail: service@dadirect.com.au

AUSTRIA
Gerold and Co.
Weihburggasse 26
A-1011 Wien
Tel: (43 1) 512-47-31-0
Fax: (43 1) 512-47-31-29

BANGLADESH
Micro Industries Development
   Assistance Society (MIDAS)
House 5, Road 16
Dhanmondi R/Area
Dhaka 1209
Tel: (880 2) 326427
Fax: (880 2) 811188

BELGIUM
Jean De Lannoy
Av. du Roi 202
1060 Brussels
Tel: (32 2) 538-5169
Fax: (32 2) 538-0841

BRAZIL
Publicações Tecnicas Internacionais Ltda.
Rua Peixoto Gomide, 209
01409 Sao Paulo, SP.
Tel: (55 11) 259-6644
Fax: (55 11) 258-6990
E-mail: postmaster@pti.uol.br

CANADA
Renouf Publishing Co. Ltd.
5369 Canotek Road
Ottawa, Ontario K1J 9J3
Tel: (613) 745-2665
Fax: (613) 745-7660
E-mail: order.dept@renoufbooks.com

CHINA
China Financial & Economic
   Publishing House
8, Da Fo Si Dong Jie
Beijing
Tel: (86 10) 6333-8257
Fax: (86 10) 6401-7365

China Book Import Centre
P.O. Box 2825
Beijing

COLOMBIA
Infoenlace Ltda.
Carrera 6 No. 51-21
Apartado Aereo 34270
Santafé de Bogotá, D.C.
Tel: (57 1) 285-2798
Fax: (57 1) 285-2798

COTE D'IVOIRE
Center d'Edition et de Diffusion Africaines
   (CEDA)
04 B.P. 541
Abidjan 04
Tel: (225) 24 6510;24 6511
Fax: (225) 25 0567

CYPRUS
Center for Applied Research
Cyprus College
6, Diogenes Street, Engomi
P.O. Box 2006
Nicosia
Tel: (357 2) 44-1730
Fax: (357 2) 46-2051

CZECH REPUBLIC
USIS, NIS Prodejna
Havelkova 22
130 00 Prague 3
Tel: (420 2) 2423 1486
Fax: (420 2) 2423 1114

DENMARK
SamfundsLitteratur
Rosenoerns Allé 11
DK-1970 Frederiksberg C
Tel: (45 31) 351942
Fax: (45 31) 357822

ECUADOR
Libri Mundi
Libreria Internacional
P.O. Box 17-01-3029
Juan Leon Mera 851
Quito
Tel: (593 2) 521-606; (593 2) 544-185
Fax: (593 2) 504-209
E-mail: librimu1@librimundi.com.ec

CODEU
Ruiz de Castilla 763, Edif. Expocolor
Primer piso, Of. #2
Quito
Tel/Fax: (593 2) 507-383; 253-091
E-mail: codeu@impsat.net.ec

EGYPT, ARAB REPUBLIC OF
Al Ahram Distribution Agency
Al Galaa Street
Cairo
Tel: (20 2) 578-6083
Fax: (20 2) 578-6833

The Middle East Observer
41, Sherif Street
Cairo
Tel: (20 2) 393-9732
Fax: (20 2) 393-9732

FINLAND
Akateeminen Kirjakauppa
P.O. Box 128
FIN-00101 Helsinki
Tel: (358 0) 121 4418
Fax: (358 0) 121-4435
E-mail: akatilaus@stockmann.fi

FRANCE
World Bank Publications
66, avenue d'Iéna
75116 Paris
Tel: (33 1) 40-69-30-56/57
Fax: (33 1) 40-69-30-68

GERMANY
UNO-Verlag
Poppelsdorfer Allee 55
53115 Bonn
Tel: (49 228) 949020
Fax: (49 228) 217492
E-mail: unoverlag@aol.com

GHANA
Epp Books Services
P.O. Box 44
TUC
Accra

GREECE
Papasotiriou S.A.
35, Stournara Str.
106 82 Athens
Tel: (30 1) 364-1826
Fax: (30 1) 364-8254

HAITI
Culture Diffusion
5, Rue Capois
C.P. 257
Port-au-Prince

HONG KONG, CHINA; MACAO
Asia 2000 Ltd.
Sales & Circulation Department
Seabird House, unit 1101-02
22-28 Wyndham Street, Central
Hong Kong
Tel: (852) 2530-1409
Fax: (852) 2526-1107
E-mail: sales@asia2000.com.hk

HUNGARY
Euro Info Service
Margitszgeti Europa Haz
H-1138 Budapest
Tel: (36 1) 350 80 24, 350 80 25
Fax: (36 1) 350 90 32
E-mail: euroinfo@mail.matav.hu

INDIA
Allied Publishers Ltd.
751 Mount Road
Madras - 600 002
Tel: (91 44) 852-3938
Fax: (91 44) 852-0649

INDONESIA
Pt. Indira Limited
Jalan Borobudur 20
P.O. Box 181
Jakarta 10320
Tel: (62 21) 390-4290
Fax: (62 21) 390-4289

IRAN
Ketab Sara Co. Publishers
Khaled Eslamboli Ave., 6th Street
Delafrooz Alley No. 8
P.O. Box 15745-733
Tehran 15117
Tel: (98 21) 8717819; 8716104
Fax: (98 21) 8712479
E-mail: ketab-sara@neda.net.ir

Kowkab Publishers
P.O. Box 19575-511
Tehran
Tel: (98 21) 258-3723
Fax: (98 21) 258-3723

IRELAND
Government Supplies Agency
Oifig an tSoláthair
4-5 Harcourt Road
Dublin 2
Tel: (353 1) 661-3111
Fax: (353 1) 475-2670

ISRAEL
Yozmot Literature Ltd.
P.O. Box 56055
3 Yohanan Hasandlar Street
Tel Aviv 61560
Tel: (972 3) 5285-397
Fax: (972 3) 5285-397

R.O.Y. International
PO Box 13056
Tel Aviv 61130
Tel: (972 3) 5461423
Fax: (972 3) 5461442
E-mail: royil@netvision.net.il

Palestinian Authority/Middle East
Index Information Services
P.O.B. 19502 Jerusalem
Tel: (972 2) 6271219
Fax: (972 2) 6271634

ITALY
Licosa Commissionaria Sansoni SPA
Via Duca Di Calabria, 1/1
Casella Postale 552
50125 Firenze
Tel: (55) 645-415
Fax: (55) 641-257
E-mail: licosa@ftbcc.it

JAMAICA
Ian Randle Publishers Ltd.
206 Old Hope Road, Kingston 6
Tel: 876-977-2085
Fax: 876-977-0243
E-mail: irpl@colis.com

JAPAN
Eastern Book Service
3-13 Hongo 3-chome, Bunkyo-ku
Tokyo 113
Tel: (81 3) 3818-0861
Fax: (81 3) 3818-0864
E-mail: orders@svt-ebs.co.jp

KENYA
Africa Book Service (E.A.) Ltd.
Quaran House, Mfangano Street
P.O. Box 45245
Nairobi
Tel: (254 2) 223 641
Fax: (254 2) 330 272

KOREA, REPUBLIC OF
Daejon Trading Co. Ltd.
P.O. Box 34, Youida, 706 Seoun Bldg
44-6 Youido-Dong, Yeongchengpo-Ku
Seoul
Tel: (82 2) 785-1631/4
Fax: (82 2) 784-0315

LEBANON
Librairie du Liban
P.O. Box 11-9232
Beirut
Tel: (961 9) 217 944
Fax: (961 9) 217 434

MALAYSIA
University of Malaya Cooperative
   Bookshop, Limited
P.O. Box 1127
Jalan Pantai Baru
59700 Kuala Lumpur
Tel: (60 3) 756-5000
Fax: (60 3) 755-4424

MEXICO
INFOTEC
Av. San Fernando No. 37
Col. Toriello Guerra
14050 Mexico, D.F.

Mundi-Prensa Mexico S.A. de C.V.
c/Rio Panuco, 141-Colonia Cuauhtemoc
06500 Mexico, D.F.
Tel: (52 5) 533-5658
Fax: (52 5) 514-6799

NEPAL
Everest Media International Services (P) Ltd.
GPO Box 5443
Kathmandu
Tel: (977 1) 472 152
Fax: (977 1) 224 431

NETHERLANDS
De Lindeboom/InOr-Publikaties
P.O. Box 202, 7480 AE Haaksbergen
Tel: (31 53) 574-0004
Fax: (31 53) 572-9296
E-mail: lindeboo@worldonline.nl

NEW ZEALAND
EBSCO NZ Ltd.
Private Mail Bag 99914
New Market
Auckland
Tel: (64 9) 524-8119
Fax: (64 9) 524-8067

NIGERIA
University Press Limited
Three Crowns Building Jericho
Private Mail Bag 5095
Ibadan
Tel: (234 22) 41-1356
Fax: (234 22) 41-2056

NORWAY
NIC Info A/S
Book Department, Postboks 6512 Etterstad
N-0606 Oslo
Tel: (47 22) 97-4500
Fax: (47 22) 97-4545

PAKISTAN
Mirza Book Agency
65, Shahrah-e-Quaid-e-Azam
Lahore 54000
Tel: (92 42) 735 3601
Fax: (92 42) 576 3714

Oxford University Press
5 Bangalore Town
Sharae Faisal
PO Box 13033
Karachi-75350
Tel: (92 21) 446307
Fax: (92 21) 4547640
E-mail: ouppak@TheOffice.net

Pak Book Corporation
Aziz Chambers 21, Queen's Road
Lahore
Tel: (92 42) 636 3222; 636 0885
Fax: (92 42) 636 2328
E-mail: pbc@brain.net.pk

PERU
Editorial Desarrollo SA
Apartado 3824, Lima 1
Tel: (51 14) 285380
Fax: (51 14) 286628

PHILIPPINES
International Booksource Center Inc.
1127-A Antipolo St. Barangay, Venezuela
Makati City
Tel: (63 2) 896 6501; 6505; 6507
Fax: (63 2) 896 1741

POLAND
International Publishing Service
Ul. Piekna 31/37
00-677 Warzawa
Tel: (48 2) 628-6089
Fax: (48 2) 621-7255
E-mail: books%ips@ikp.atm.com.pl

PORTUGAL
Livraria Portugal
Apartado 2681, Rua Do Carmo 70-74
1200 Lisbon
Tel: (1) 347-4982
Fax: (1) 347-0264

ROMANIA
Compani De Librarii Bucuresti S.A.
Str. Lipscani no. 26, sector 3
Bucharest
Tel: (40 1) 613 9645
Fax: (40 1) 312 4000

RUSSIAN FEDERATION
Isdatelstvo <Ves Mir>
9a, Kolpachniy Pereulok
Moscow 101831
Tel: (7 095) 917 87 49
Fax: (7 095) 917 92 59

**SINGAPORE; TAIWAN, CHINA;
MYANMAR; BRUNEI**
Ashgate Publishing Asia Pacific Pte. Ltd.
41 Kallang Pudding Road #04-03
Golden Wheel Building
Singapore 349316
Tel: (65) 741-5166
Fax: (65) 742-9356
E-mail: ashgate@asianconnect.com

SLOVENIA
Gospodarski Vestnik Publishing Group
Dunajska cesta 5
1000 Ljubljana
Tel: (386 61) 133 83 47; 132 12 30
Fax: (386 61) 133 80 30
E-mail: repansekj@gvestnik.si

SOUTH AFRICA, BOTSWANA
For single titles:
Oxford University Press Southern Africa
Vasco Boulevard, Goodwood
P.O. Box 12119, N1 City 7463
Cape Town
Tel: (27 21) 595 4400
Fax: (27 21) 595 4430
E-mail: oxford@oup.co.za

For subscription orders:
International Subscription Service
P.O. Box 41095
Craighall
Johannesburg 2024
Tel: (27 11) 880-1448
Fax: (27 11) 880-6248
E-mail: iss@is.co.za

SPAIN
Mundi-Prensa Libros, S.A.
Castello 37
28001 Madrid
Tel: (34 1) 431-3399
Fax: (34 1) 575-3998
E-mail: libreria@mundiprensa.es

Mundi-Prensa Barcelona
Consell de Cent, 391
08009 Barcelona
Tel: (34 3) 488-3492
Fax: (34 3) 487-7659
E-mail: barcelona@mundiprensa.es

SRI LANKA, THE MALDIVES
Lake House Bookshop
100, Sir Chittampalam Gardiner Mawatha
Colombo 2
Tel: (94 1) 32105

Fax: (94 1) 432104
E-mail: LHL@sri.lanka.net

SWEDEN
Wennergren-Williams AB
P.O. Box 1305
S-171 25 Solna
Tel: (46 8) 705-97-50
Fax: (46 8) 27-00-71
E-mail: mail@wwi.se

SWITZERLAND
Librairie Payot Service Institutionnel
Côtes-de-Montbenon 30
1002 Lausanne
Tel: (41 21) 341-3229
Fax: (41 21) 341-3235

ADECO Van Diermen EditionsTechniques
Ch. de Lacuez 41
CH1807 Blonay
Tel: (41 21) 943 2673
Fax: (41 21) 943 3605

THAILAND
Central Books Distribution
306 Silom Road
Bangkok 10500
Tel: (66 2) 235-5400
Fax: (66 2) 237-8321

**TRINIDAD & TOBAGO
AND THE CARRIBBEAN**
Systematics Studies Ltd.
St. Augustine Shopping Center
Eastern Main Road, St. Augustine
Trinidad & Tobago, West Indies
Tel: (868) 645-8466
Fax: (868) 645-8467
E-mail: tobe@trinidad.net

UGANDA
Gustro Ltd.
PO Box 9997, Madhvani Building
Plot 16/4 Jinja Rd.
Kampala
Tel: (256 41) 251 467
Fax: (256 41) 251 468
E-mail: gus@swiftuganda.com

UNITED KINGDOM
Microinfo Ltd.
P.O. Box 3, Alton, Hampshire GU34 2PG
England
Tel: (44 1420) 86848
Fax: (44 1420) 89889
E-mail: wbank@ukminfo.demon.co.uk

The Stationery Office
51 Nine Elms Lane
London SW8 5DR
Tel: (44 171) 873-8400
Fax: (44 171) 873-8242

VENEZUELA
Tecni-Ciencia Libros, S.A.
Centro Cuidad Comercial Tamanco
Nivel C2, Caracas
Tel: (58 2) 959 5547; 5035; 0016
Fax: (58 2) 959 5636

ZAMBIA
University Bookshop, University of Zambia
Great East Road Campus
P.O. Box 32379
Lusaka
Tel: (260 1) 252 576
Fax: (260 1) 253 952

ZIMBABWE
Academic and Baobab Books (Pvt.) Ltd.
4 Conald Road, Graniteside
P.O. Box 567
Harare
Tel: 263 4 755035
Fax: 263 4 781913